25 Holiday & Seasonal

Emergent Reader Mini-Books

◆◆◆◆◆◆◆◆◆◆◆◆◆ by Maria Fleming ◆◆◆◆◆◆◆◆◆◆◆◆◆

SCHOLASTIC
PROFESSIONAL BOOKS

NEW YORK • TORONTO • LONDON • AUCKLAND • SYDNEY

Cover design by Pamela Simmons
Cover photos by Donnelly Marks
Cover and interior illustrations by Anne Kennedy
Interior design by Kathy Massaro

ISBN # 0-590-10616-3
Copyright © 1998 by Maria Fleming
Printed in the U.S.A.

Contents

SEPTEMBER

OCTOBER

NOVEMBER

DECEMBER

JANUARY

FEBRUARY

MARCH

APRIL

MAY

JUNE

OTHER CELEBRATIONS

Introduction

*L*iterature is always a great way to introduce a holiday celebration. What better choice than books even the youngest students can read themselves! Here are reproducible patterns to make 25 mini-books to develop and support students' reading skills as they celebrate holidays and seasonal events. This book includes stories for month-by-month celebrations— from the first day of school to the last.

You'll find that the mini-books have myriad uses in your reading program. Use them for shared reading, guided reading, paired or independent reading. Record the text on an audiotape, and place the book and recording in a holiday-themed learning center. Tuck the mini-books into backpacks so students can keep celebrating—and reading—at home.

The books are easy to make and easy to read—they contain predictable language, rhymes, and repetition to help children gain confidence as readers and develop fluency. While all of the books are designed for emergent readers, they vary slightly in degree of difficulty. You may want to begin each book as a shared reading experience. Working with the whole class, model a reading strategy as you move through the text of the book. For example, you might demonstrate how readers can rely on picture clues or context cues to help decode text. Or you might isolate a phonics skill and offer a mini-lesson on it.

Background information on the holidays and activities to launch or follow up your mini-book readings are included on pages 6–14. The stories and activities can be used to enrich students' understanding of our nation's history, multicultural traditions, and the changing seasons. The activities, while intended to be fun, will help give your readings and holiday celebrations cross-curricular mileage.

I hope these mini-books will help make reading an everyday celebratory event in your classroom.

Happy holidays. And happy reading!

Maria Fleming

Celebration Activities

SEPTEMBER

SO LONG, SUMMER!

Here's a **back-to-school** story to kick off a year of celebrations. After students read the story, make a class chart divided into two columns, labeled "What I'll Miss About Summer" and "What I'm Looking Forward to This School Year," respectively. This charting activity will serve a dual function by creating an opportunity to discuss what children did over the summer months and to set goals for the upcoming school year.

ONE LITTLE PUMPKIN

Pumpkins ripening in patches signal **autumn's arrival** on September 21. After reading this simple counting rhyme, invite children to participate in a variety of pumpkin-math activities using real pumpkins and gourds:

- If you have enough pumpkins, students can use the fruit to "act out" the counting rhyme.

- Use the pumpkins for size comparisons, exploring the concepts of big, bigger, biggest and small, smaller, smallest.

- Ask children to classify the pumpkins into groups according to various characteristics (size, color, or other attributes).

- Pick the largest pumpkin and ask students to estimate its weight and/or number of seeds.

- Steam-cook a pumpkin and scrape out its flesh and seeds. Students can practice their measuring skills as they prepare a pumpkin-flavored dish, such as pudding or muffins, using the cooked pumpkin meat. And the clean, dried seeds make good math manipulatives and are a yummy snack when toasted in the oven!

JOHNNY APPLESEED'S GIFT

Johnny Appleseed Day, celebrated on September 26, honors the birthday of John Chapman, who was born in Leominster, Massachusetts, in 1774. The farm where he was raised had many apple trees, and when John was 20, he strapped a bag of apple seeds over his shoulder and set out to spread the bounty. He wandered across the frontier, planting apple seeds wherever he saw settlers. People said the friendly man in ragged clothes wore his cooking pot on his head to keep his hands free for whatever book he was reading.

Explain to students why Johnny was enthusiastically greeted wherever he went: Apples were used by settlers for eating, making cider, and cooking different dishes. To commemorate this special day, students may enjoy collecting their favorite apple recipes from home and from school staff members. Students can compile their recipes into an apple-shaped book. They may want to pick one or two recipes—for example, applesauce cake and hot apple cider—to serve at a birthday party honoring John Chapman.

OCTOBER

WHAT SHOULD I BE FOR HALLOWEEN?

The custom of dressing up for **Halloween** began some 2,000 years ago with the ancient Celts, who donned animal skins or other costumes so that evil spirits would not recognize them. Provide children with large paper plates and a variety of craft materials (colored paper, glitter, yarn, tissue paper, beads, sequins, feathers, paints, and so on), and invite them to make the simplest of Halloween costumes: masks. After students cut out eyeholes and mouth holes, show them how to tie the masks on with string. Then hold a miniature Halloween costume parade and march through the school halls.

NOTE: Before doing this activity, you may want to send a letter home to parents to be certain the celebration of Halloween doesn't conflict with the religious beliefs of children's families.

How to Make the Mini-Books

1. Copy the pages for the books on standard 8 1/2-by-11-inch paper, making single-sided copies.

2. Trim off the shaded edge of each page. Then cut apart the mini-book pages along the solid lines. You should have 8 pages (including the cover) for each book.

3. Put the pages in order with the cover on top. Staple the pages on the left side to make the book.

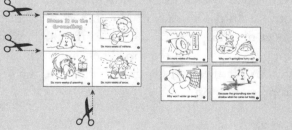

PEANUT BUTTER IS DELICIOUS

Peanut Butter Day, a day set aside to honor that stick-to-the-roof-of-your-mouth sandwich favorite, is celebrated on November 13. Students can follow the simple recipe below to make homemade peanut butter. After reading the story, ask children to share their favorite way to eat peanut butter. Then plan a peanut butter sampling party, during which students can try the homemade peanut butter on some of the items they named. Students can vote on their favorite way to enjoy this nutritious and delicious food and graph the results.

Ingredients:

- 4 cups dry roasted peanuts (unsalted)
- 2 tablespoons peanut oil
- 2 teaspoons sugar
- salt (to taste, about a teaspoon)

1. Put all the ingredients in a blender or food processor.
2. Pulse at high speed until the peanuts become smooth. (You'll need to stop the blender or food processor a couple of times to scrape down the sides.)

READ, READ, READ A BOOK

This story-song will help motivate children to keep reading during **National Book Week**—celebrated during the third week of November—and all year long. Present children with a book-week reading challenge. Divide the class into teams of four and see which team can read the most books in seven days. Encourage students, as the mini-book suggests, to read with any and everyone who will sit still for a story! Create a picture graph using simple book-shaped icons to keep track of team totals.

TODAY WE GIVE THANKS

What will your students be thankful for this **Thanksgiving Day,** celebrated on the third Thursday in November? After reading the story, spread a long sheet of craft paper on a table or the floor. Write "Today We Give Thanks for _____" across the top. Then invite children to make a collage of cutout pictures and words that illustrate the people and things they appreciate most.

December

Sledding Song

The December 21 **arrival of winter** means snow in some parts of the country, and snow means winter fun. After students read and/or sing this story-song, they may enjoy making a big book titled after the refrain, "Winter Is So Much Fun!" Ask children each to contribute a page by drawing a picture of themselves engaged in a favorite winter activity. Students can write or dictate sentences about their pictures before binding the pages together.

December Is Time to Celebrate

This mini-book offers a glimpse at some of the traditions associated with three December holidays:

- **Hanukkah** usually falls in December. (It varies year to year according to the Jewish calendar.) It is an eight-day Jewish holiday commemorating the triumph of the Maccabees over the army of the Syrian king, Antiochus IV. Among Hanukkah traditions is the lighting of the *menorah* (page 2 of book), which symbolizes the miracle of the oil that burned for eight days when the victorious Maccabees rededicated the temple that had been seized by Antiochus. Potato pancakes (page 4), called *latkes*, are a special holiday treat.

- **Christmas,** a Christian holiday celebrating the birth of Jesus Christ, is celebrated on December 25. Trimming trees (page 3), a custom originated by a German monk in the eighth century, and singing carols (page 6), another old European tradition, are usually part of the festivities.

- **Kwanzaa,** a celebration of African American heritage, begins on December 26 and ends on January 1. Each day, families light one of the candles, called *mishumaa saba* (mee-shoo-MAH-ah SAH-bah), in a special candleholder called a *kinara* (kee-NAH-rah), shown on page 7. Each candle represents one of the seven Kwanzaa principles: unity, purpose, creativity, faith, self-determination, collective work and responsibility, and cooperative economics. Families often wear African-inspired dress (page 5) and conduct a special ceremony around the Kwanzaa table (page 7). The ceremony involves various symbolic items placed on a straw mat, called a *mkeka* (em-KAY-kah). A bowl of fruit and vegetables, called the *mazao* (mah-ZAH-oh), represents the harvest. Ears of corn, called *muhindi* (moo-HIN-dee), represent children and the future.

You may want to explain some of the history and traditions of these holidays to children before they read the story. Ask students what holidays, if any, they celebrate in December. Invite family members into class to share and explain their holiday traditions. Plan a special holiday party that incorporates the traditions of all religious and cultural groups in the class.

JANUARY

WELCOME IN THE NEW YEAR

This rhyming story cries out for accompanying sound effects to herald the arrival of **New Year's Day** on January 1. Divide the class into seven small groups, and assign each group a "sound role"—for example, bell-ringers, pan-clangers, and so on. Provide props as necessary. As you read the story together, groups can jump in on their respective cues and offer the appropriate sound effect. On the final page, cue all groups for a cacophonous culmination to the rhyme!

HE HAD A DREAM

After sharing this story to commemorate **Martin Luther King, Jr.'s Birthday** on January 15, read aloud to students King's famous "I Have a Dream" speech. Then create a special birthday bulletin board display in King's honor. Cut out a large cake shape from oaktag. Enlist children's help to decorate it to look like a birthday cake. Write "Happy Birthday, Dr. King" on top. Then provide each child with a simple birthday candle pattern. Ask children to write their own dreams and wishes for the world on the candles. Staple the candles to the top of the cake.

DANCE, DRAGON, DANCE

Chinese New Year falls on the first day of the new moon, usually between January 21 and February 20. It is a time designated for giving thanks for the preceding year and getting ready for the new year. Preparations may include cleaning the house, buying and wearing new clothes, paying debts, and cooking special foods. During Chinese New Year, people greet each other with "Gung hay fat choy!," which means "Wishing you to prosper."

The New Year's celebration, which can run a week or longer, culminates in the Feast of Lanterns, in which a parade of lantern-bearing marchers follow an enormous dancing dragon. Myth holds that the dragon, the Chinese symbol of strength and goodness, has been hibernating all year and has awakened for the New Year's celebration. Following the parade, the dragon will fall asleep again until the next new year.

Children can decorate a large cardboard box to resemble a dragon's head. Incorporate bright streamers; fabric; sequins; and other colorful, flashy materials into the design. Cut a flap away from the front of the box so that the student who will wear it can see. On a specified day, ask children to wear orange, red, or yellow tops (traditional holiday colors). Have five or six students form a line, holding each other by the waist. The child at the head of the line dons the dragon's head. Challenge students to dance ensemble, with the first child leading the chain in twisting, turning, rhythmic movements. The rest of the class can recite the words of the mini-book as a chant to accompany the dancing. Let all students have a turn performing.

FEBRUARY

BLAME IT ON THE GROUNDHOG

Folklore has it that if a groundhog sees its shadow when it emerges on February 2—**Groundhog Day**—there will be six more weeks of icy weather. If the groundhog doesn't see its shadow, an early spring is supposedly on its way.

Assist children in making pop-up groundhog cup puppets. For a scientific approach to this whimsical holiday, students can use their cup puppets to explore how shadows are made.

Materials (for each student)
paint, paintbrushes, paper cup, glue, groundhog pattern (right), oaktag, scissors, crayons, craft stick

1. Paint the cup brown and let it dry.

2. Glue a copy of the groundhog pattern onto oaktag and cut it out.

3. Color the groundhog a dark color.

4. Use the craft stick to poke a hole through the bottom of the paper cup.

5. Glue the groundhog pattern to one end of the craft stick; push the other end through the hole.

6. Push up and pull down on the stick to simulate the groundhog popping in and out of its hole.

Groundhog pattern

MADE WITH LOVE

No **Valentine's Day** celebration would be complete without pastel-colored candy conversation hearts. Here's a trio of activities to make math on Valentine's Day a sweet experience. (Be sure to have extra hearts on hand for nibbling!)

Made With Love

● Display a large jarful of hearts, and invite students to estimate how many hearts it contains. Encourage them to share the strategies they used in making their estimations.

● Use the hearts as manipulatives with a counting mat. Have children count by twos, fives, and tens. Use the hearts to help visualize the number 100.

● Divide the class into small groups, and provide each group with a large handful of hearts. Ask students to classify them in different ways—by color, by message, or by number of words in the message.

GEORGE WASHINGTON LOVED HIS COUNTRY

Have students use the mini-book as a model for writing a story about the boyhood of the other great leader honored on **Presidents' Day** (celebrated on the third Monday in February). You may first want to read aloud books about Abraham Lincoln's childhood to provide students with background information. A good one to introduce our sixteenth president to children is *Young Abraham Lincoln: The Frontier Days, 1809–1837* by Cheryl Harness (National Geographic Society, 1996). If students are interested in learning more about George Washington's life as a boy, as well as his life as a general and president, *George Washington: A Picture Book Biography* by James Cross Giblin (Scholastic, 1992) is a thorough and engaging resource.

MARCH

HAVE YOU SEEN MY POT OF GOLD?

Leprechauns, shamrocks, and green *everything* are the order of the day on March 17, **St. Patrick's Day**, which honors the patron saint of Ireland. This mini-book readily lends itself to theatrical adaptation. Divide the class into small groups. Assist groups in making finger or stick puppets of the characters in the story. (Stick puppets can be created easily by making enlarged photocopies of the mini-book pages, coloring and cutting out the characters, and taping them to craft sticks.) Students can also create a simple shoe-box stage or poster-board scenery to use as a backdrop for their story retellings.

SPRING IS HERE!

Welcome the March 21 **arrival of spring** and warmer weather by planting sunflowers! Have children fill eggshell halves (cleaned and dried) with soil. Plant a seed in each eggshell and sprinkle with water. Carefully place the eggshell planters in empty egg cartons. Cover the cartons with plastic wrap, and place in a dark spot. Keep soil moist, but not too wet. When the seeds sprout, move the cartons to the windowsill. In a few weeks, transfer the seedlings outside, planting them (still in eggshells) in a sunny spot. Have children record their observations in science journals as their seeds grow and change.

APRIL

GUESS WHAT I SAW TODAY!

Good-natured jokes and harmless pranks are customary on **April Fool's Day**, which falls on April 1 and kicks off **National Laugh Week**. After students read the story, help keep them giggling by compiling a classroom compendium of favorite jokes and riddles. You may want to prepare the joke and riddle book—complete with student-drawn illustrations—prior to the holiday so you'll have it on hand to share with other classes on April 1.

WHO NEEDS A TREE?

The celebration of **Earth Day,** which falls on April 22, began in 1970 and grew out of concern for the environment. Earth Day is viewed as an occasion to raise awareness about protecting against air and water pollution, preserving natural resources, and basically keeping our planet clean and green.

Have students work as a class to compose an acrostic poem that pays tribute to the earth, with each letter of the word beginning a line. Write the poem on a banner and display it on your classroom door as a reminder to others to take care of our planet. Alternatively, students may want to compose a pledge to be good "earthkeepers" and write it on a banner for display. Students can "sign" the pledge with mud handprints for an earthy touch.

MAY

BE KIND TO FURRY FRIENDS

The first week of May is designated as **Be Kind to Animals Week.** Invite a veterinarian or zookeeper to your classroom to speak with students about animal behavior and/or proper pet care. Before the visit, have children prepare a list of questions.

As a surprise for their guest, students may want to hold a paper-bag pet show. A day or two before the visit, provide students with paper lunch bags and a variety of art materials (including pipe cleaners, fabric scraps, wiggle eyes, paint, yarn, and so on). After children decorate the bags to resemble popular pets, stuff the bags with crumpled newspaper and staple them shut. Attach oaktag "feet" so that the critters can stand up.

FIESTA!

Cinco de Mayo—which translates as May 5—commemorates the Mexican victory in 1862 over invading French troops that were trying to capture Mexico City and seize control of the country. The day is celebrated in Mexico and throughout the southwestern United States and southern California with battle reenactments, parades, fireworks, and huge parties, or fiestas.

Plan a classroom fiesta for Cinco de Mayo with a make-your-own-taco theme. Ask parent volunteers to help supply food. Family members can also help children make colorful tissue-paper flowers, a traditional Mexican decoration, to display around the classroom. A colorful Mexican blanket, if anyone has one to loan you, also makes a festive wall decoration. Obtain some mariachi music to play, and you're ready to fiesta!

JUNE

A JUNE MYSTERY

Use the mini-book story and the occasion of **Flag Day** on June 14 to launch a social studies lesson about the symbolism of our flag's color and patterns. (Red symbolizes courage; white, purity; and blue, justice. Each stripe represents one of the first 13 states; each star represents a current state.) Discuss how and why the design of the flag has evolved.

SCHOOL'S OUT!

End the school year on the right note with this story-song that celebrates the last day of school. After reading the story together, divide the class into three large groups and ask each group to sing a part of the song in sequence. Prior to the last day of school, assist children in making simple autograph books. Students may want to use favorite pieces of artwork from their portfolios to make decorative front and back covers.

OTHER CELEBRATIONS

PUT ON YOUR PARTY HAT

This mini-book can be read in honor of any student or classroom visitor celebrating a **birthday**. Just fill in the name of the celebrant on the last page of the book.

Encourage students to let their imaginations loose as they create festive party hats. Students can make simple cone-shaped hats from oaktag. Provide a variety of craft materials, and allow children to decorate the hats in any fanciful way their heart desires—for example, with streamers cascading from the top, a big feathered plume, glue-on button polka dots, and so on. Store the completed hats for future celebrations.

GIFTS ARE GREAT

This mini-book can be used to launch a **birthday celebration** or to introduce any **gift-giving holiday**. After reading about how great it is to get gifts, students can write about how great it is to give them. Ask children to think of a special person in their life. If they could give that person anything in the world—from a trinket at the mall to the moon in the sky—what would it be, and why? Help students express their thoughts in free-form poetry.

The poems themselves can then become lovely birthday, holiday, or any-day gifts. Provide each student with a plain paper lunch bag. Students can decorate the bags with paints or other materials, such as commercial ink-pad stamps, potato prints, stickers, and so on. Put each poem in a bag. Fold down the top about 1/2 inch and staple it shut. Hole punch the top of the bag and tie a ribbon through it. Children can present their poems to the special people they wrote about.

So Long, Summer!

1 So long to sand castles.

2 So long to seashells.

3 So long to watermelon.

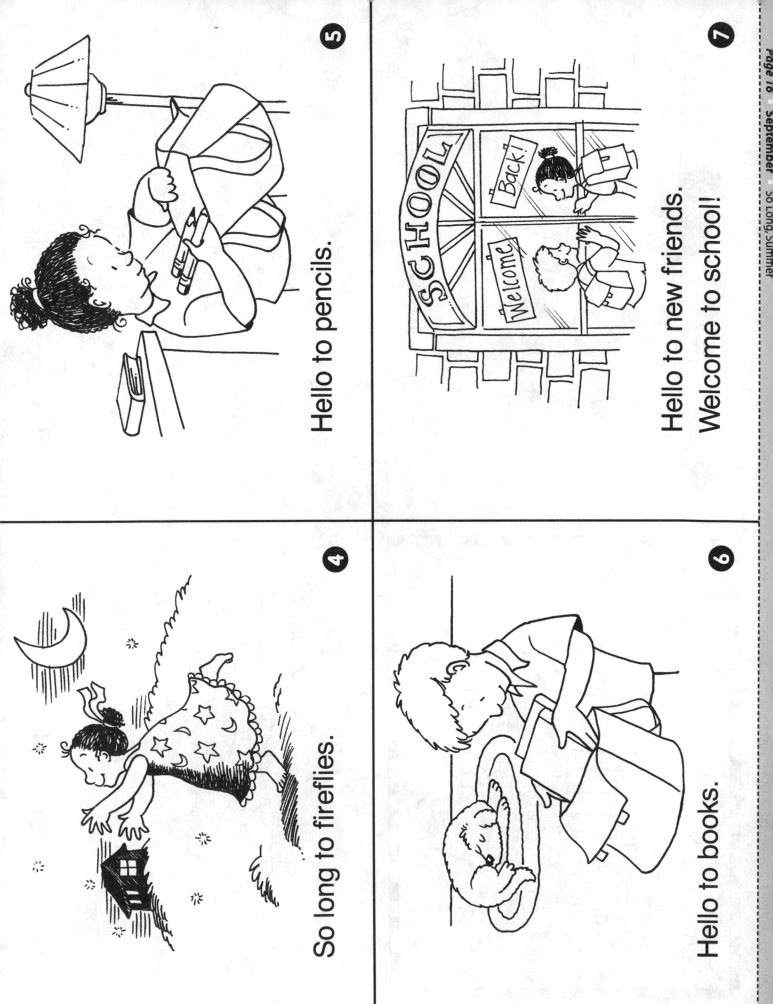

7

Hello to new friends.
Welcome to school!

5

Hello to pencils.

6

Hello to books.

4

So long to fireflies.

One Little Pumpkin

(Sing to the tune of "Ten Little Indians")

1 One little, two little, three little pumpkins,

2 four little, five little, six little pumpkins,

3 seven little, eight little, nine little pumpkins, ten pumpkins growing in a patch.

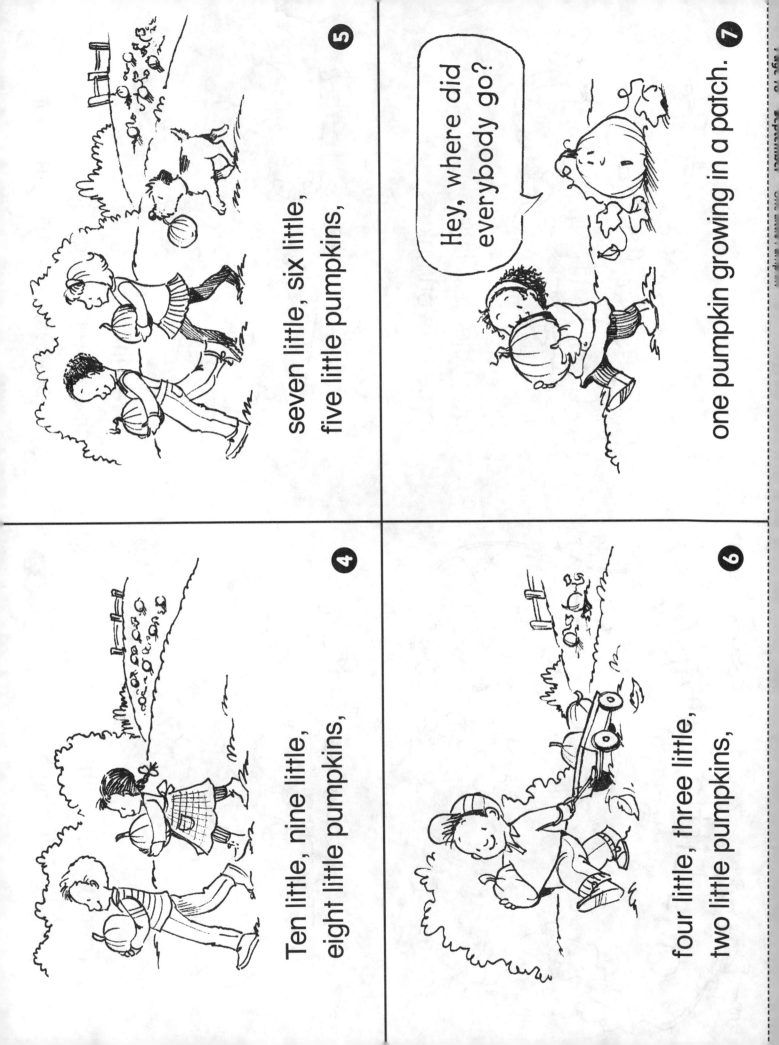

4

Ten little, nine little, eight little pumpkins,

5

seven little, six little, five little pumpkins,

6

four little, three little, two little pumpkins,

7

one pumpkin growing in a patch.

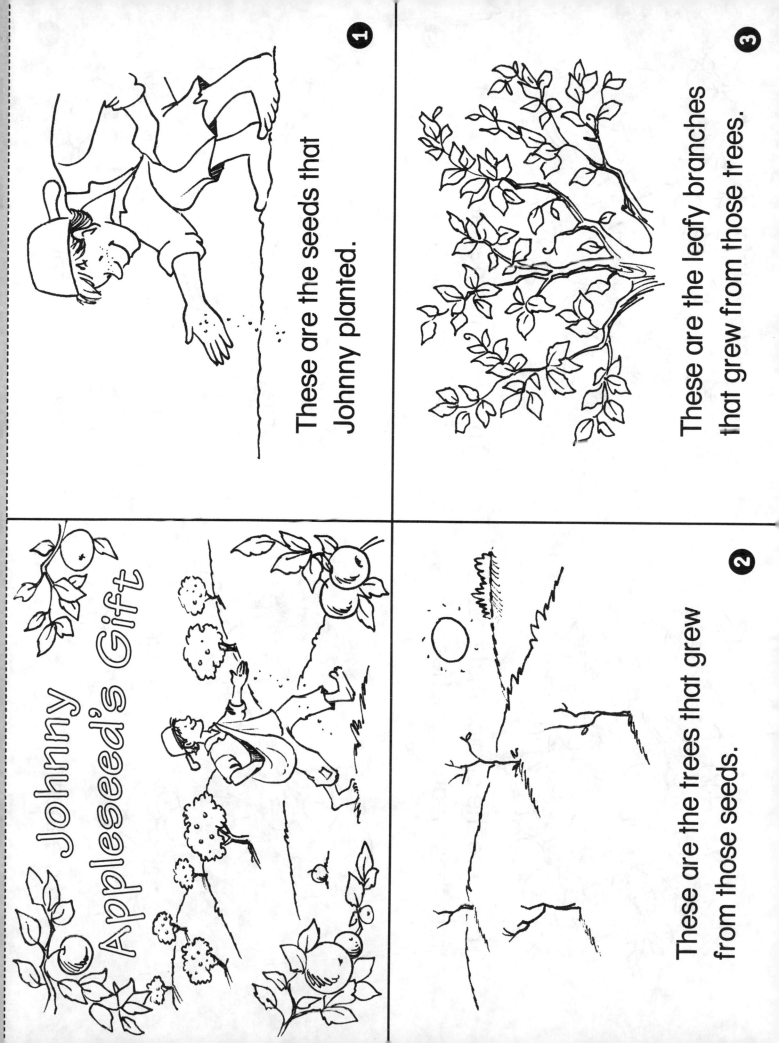

1

These are the seeds that Johnny planted.

3

These are the leafy branches that grew from those trees.

Johnny Appleseed's Gift

2

These are the trees that grew from those seeds.

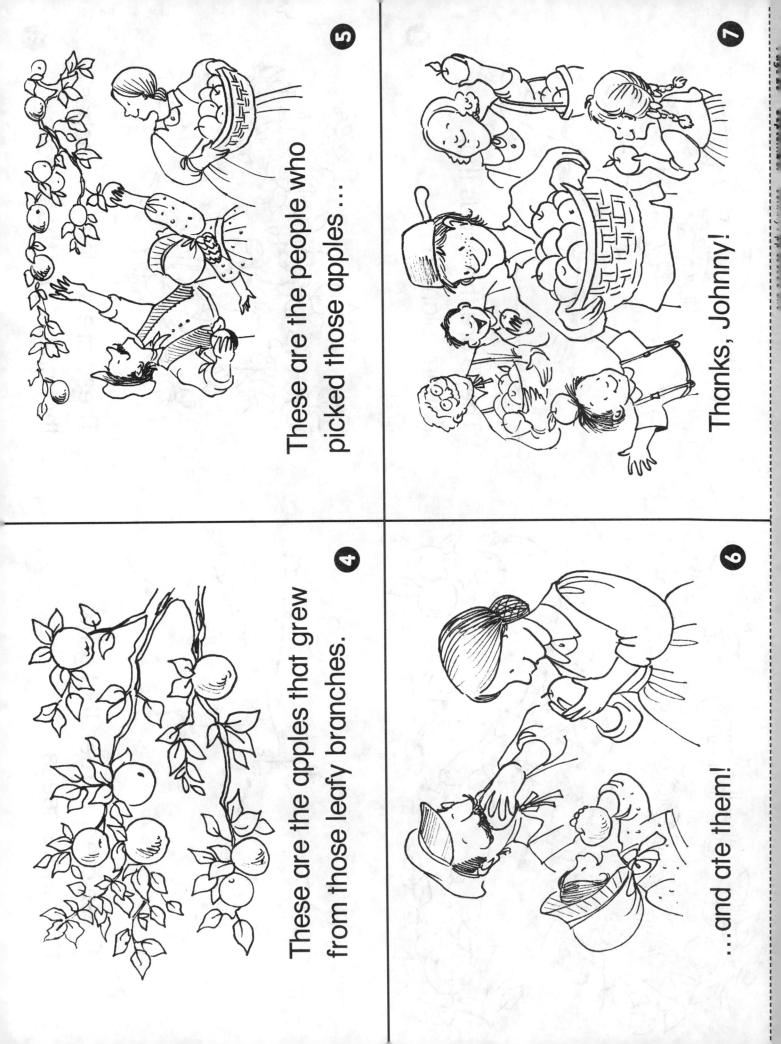

5

These are the people who
picked those apples ...

7

Thanks, Johnny!

4

These are the apples that grew
from those leafy branches.

6

...and ate them!

What Should I Be
for Halloween?

1

Maybe I'll be a clown.

2

Maybe I'll be a tree.

3

Maybe I'll be a pirate.

Maybe I'll be a firefighter.

Today I can be ANYTHING, just not myself!

Maybe I'll be a bee.

Maybe I'll be an elf.

Peanut Butter Is Delicious

1

Peanut butter is delicious on bread.

2

Peanut butter is delicious on crackers.

3

Peanut butter is delicious on celery.

5 Peanut butter is delicious on an apple.

7 Well, maybe not on a hot dog!

4 Peanut butter is delicious on a banana.

6 Peanut butter is delicious on a hot dog.

1

Read, read, read a book,
to anyone you wish.

3

Read one to your fish.

Read, Read, Read a Book

(Sing to the tune of "Row, Row, Row Your Boat")

2

Read one to your cat or dog.

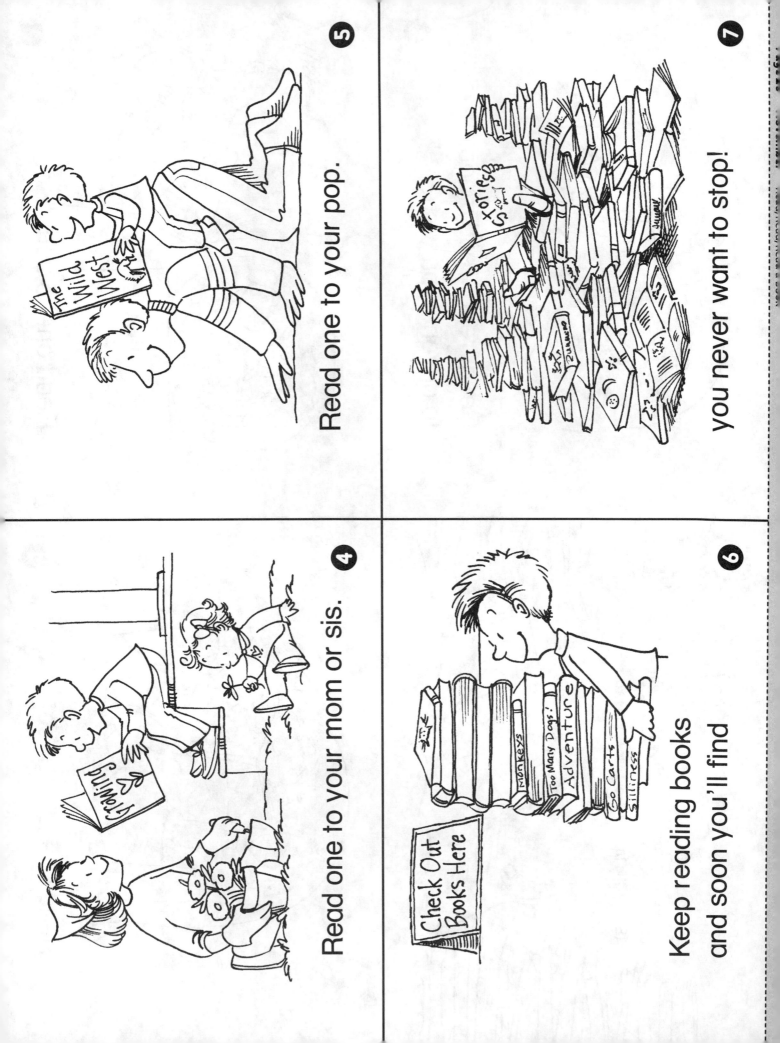

5

Read one to your pop.

7

you never want to stop!

4

Read one to your mom or sis.

6

Keep reading books
and soon you'll find

Today we give thanks for families.

Today we give thanks for cozy beds.

Today We
Give Thanks

Today we give thanks for warm clothes.

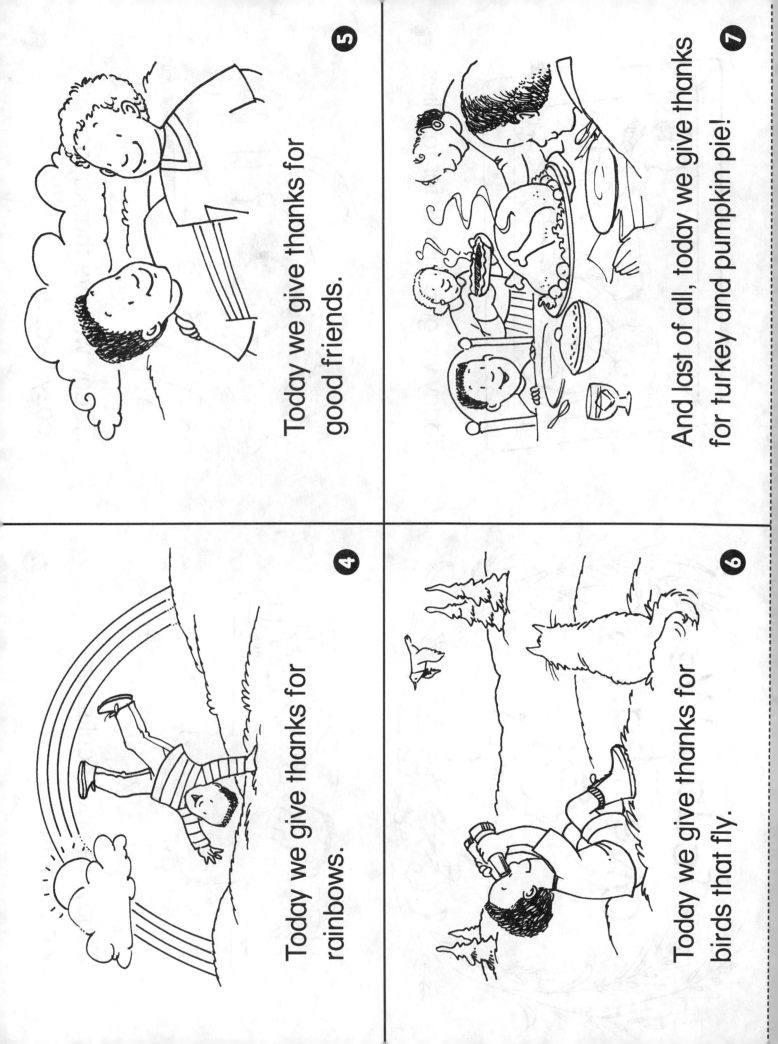

5

Today we give thanks for good friends.

7

And last of all, today we give thanks for turkey and pumpkin pie!

4

Today we give thanks for rainbows.

6

Today we give thanks for birds that fly.

Sledding Song

(Sing to the tune of "Here We Go 'Round the Mulberry Bush")

1

Here we go marching through the snow,
through the snow, through the snow.

2

Here we go marching through the snow.
Winter is so much fun!

3

Here we go climbing up the hill,
up the hill, up the hill.

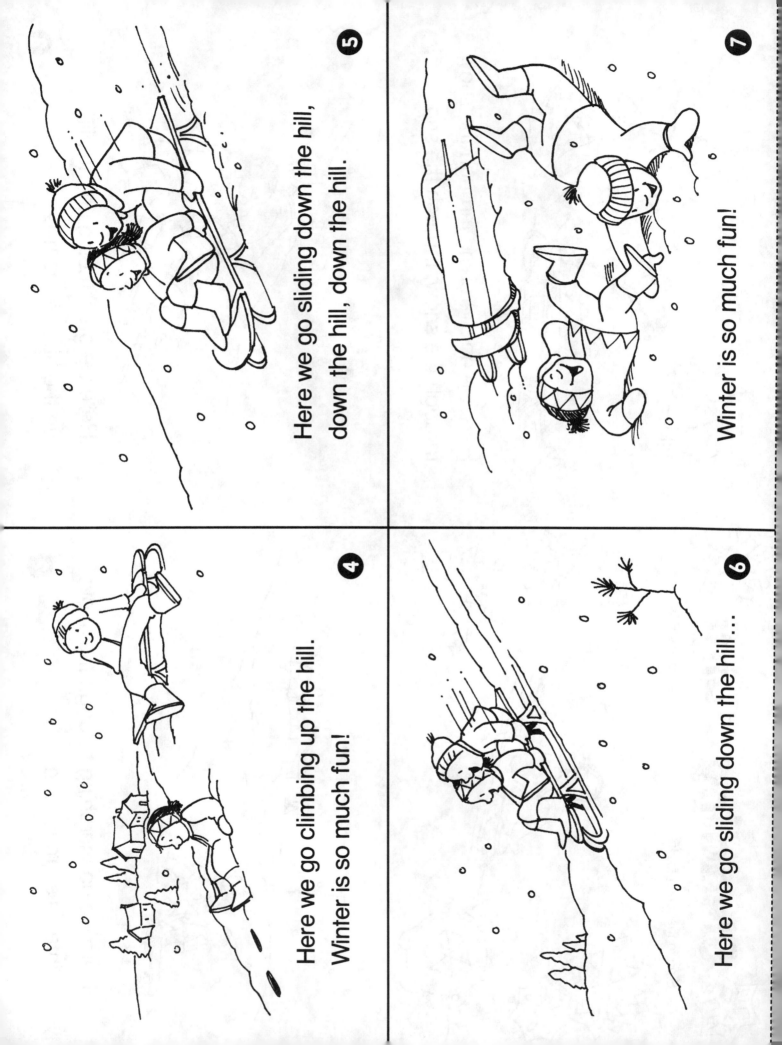

5

Here we go sliding down the hill,
down the hill, down the hill.

7

Winter is so much fun!

4

Here we go climbing up the hill.
Winter is so much fun!

6

Here we go sliding down the hill....

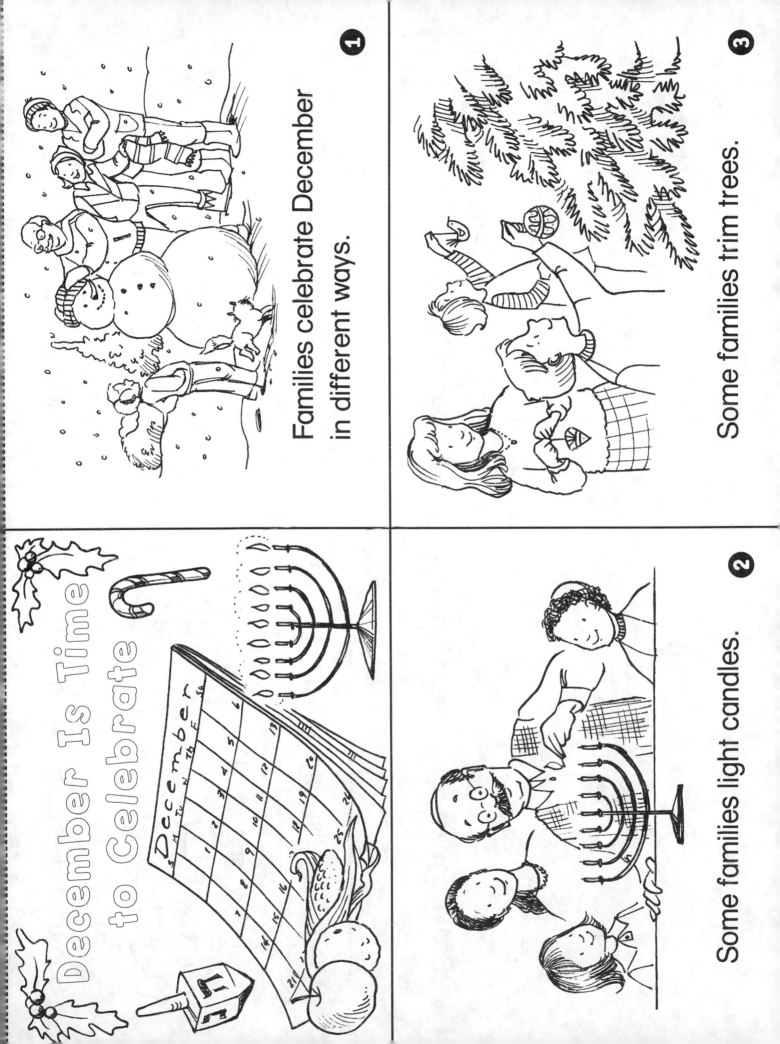

December Is Time to Celebrate

Families celebrate December in different ways.

1

Some families light candles.

2

Some families trim trees.

3

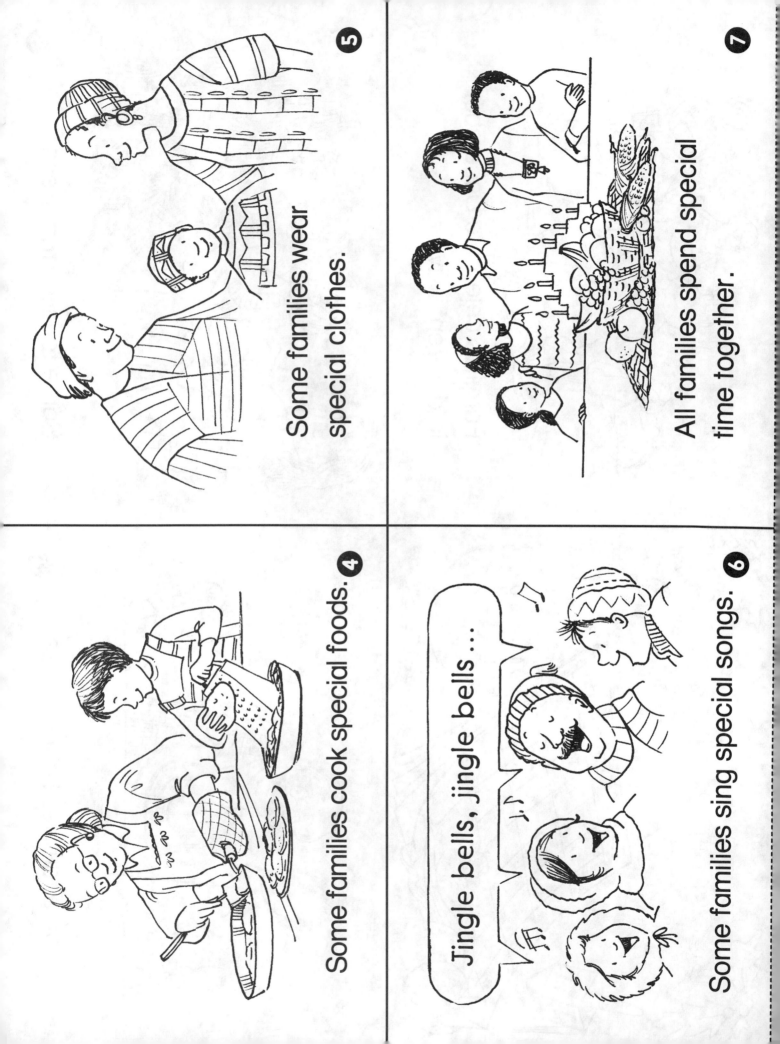

5

Some families wear special clothes.

7

All families spend special time together.

4

Some families cook special foods.

6

Jingle bells, jingle bells …

Some families sing special songs.

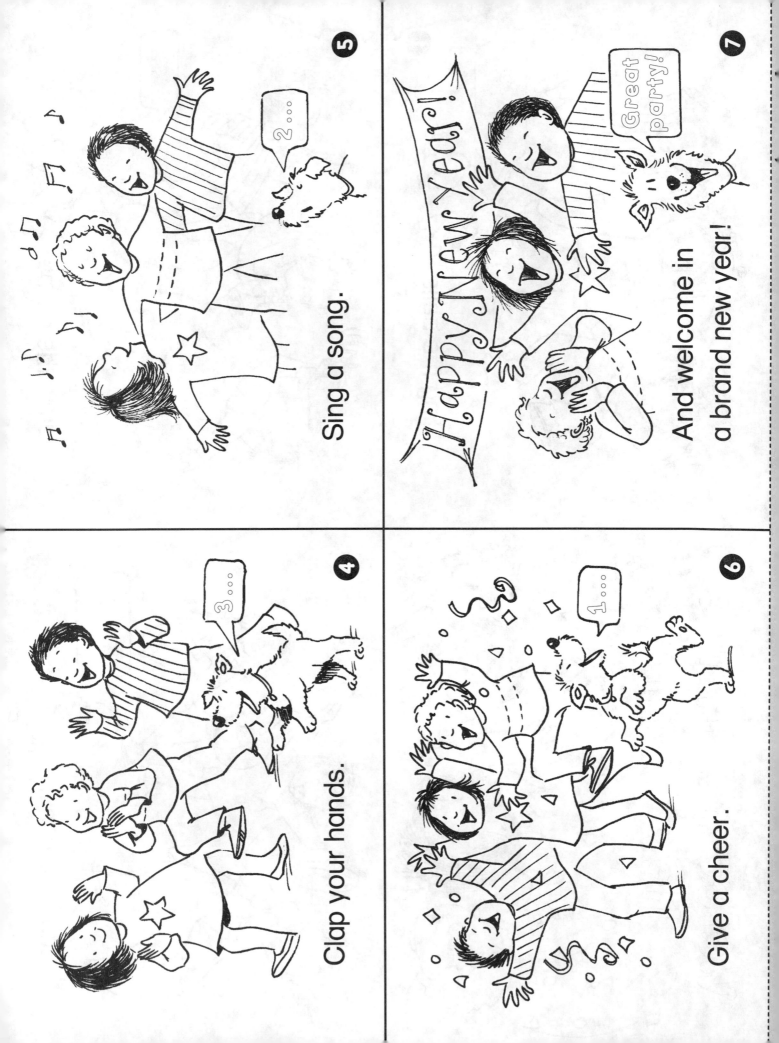

5 Sing a song.

7 And welcome in a brand new year!

4 Clap your hands.

6 Give a cheer.

1

Martin Luther King, Jr., gave us a gift.
His gift was a dream.

3

Neighborhood **Picnic**
Here on Saturday

They would work together.

He Had a Dream

2

Are you going to the picnic tomorrow?

Of course.

He dreamed that people of all colors would get along.

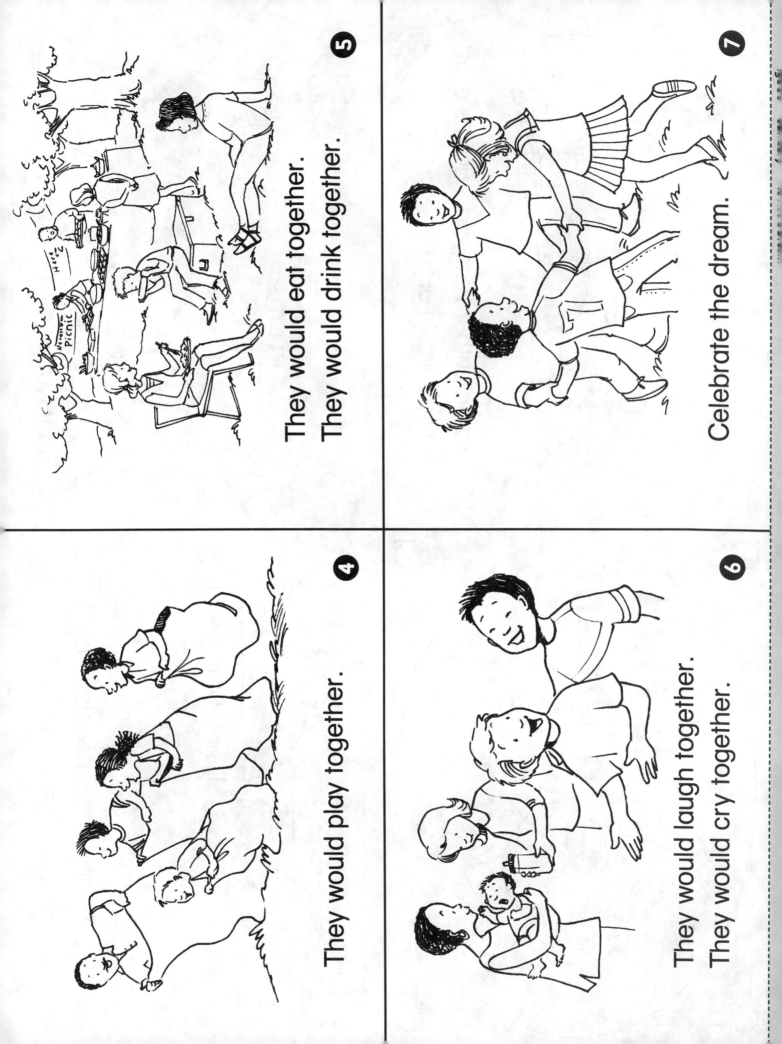

5

They would eat together.
They would drink together.

7

Celebrate the dream.

4

They would play together.

6

They would laugh together.
They would cry together.

1

Tonight the dragon will dance.
Dance, dragon, dance.

3

Dance past the shops.
Dance, dragon, dance.

Dance, Dragon, Dance

2

Dance through the street.
Dance, dragon, dance.

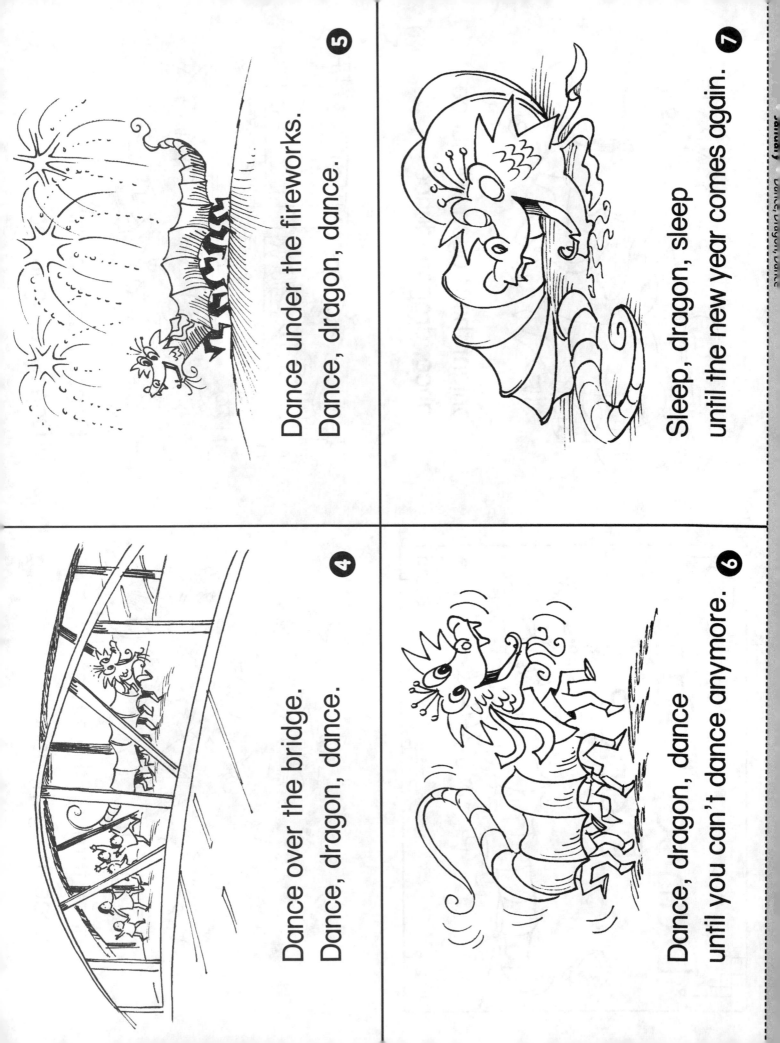

5

Dance under the fireworks.
Dance, dragon, dance.

7

Sleep, dragon, sleep
until the new year comes again.

4

Dance over the bridge.
Dance, dragon, dance.

6

Dance, dragon, dance
until you can't dance anymore.

Blame It on the Groundhog

1

Six more weeks of mittens.

2

Six more weeks of sneezing.

3

Six more weeks of snow.

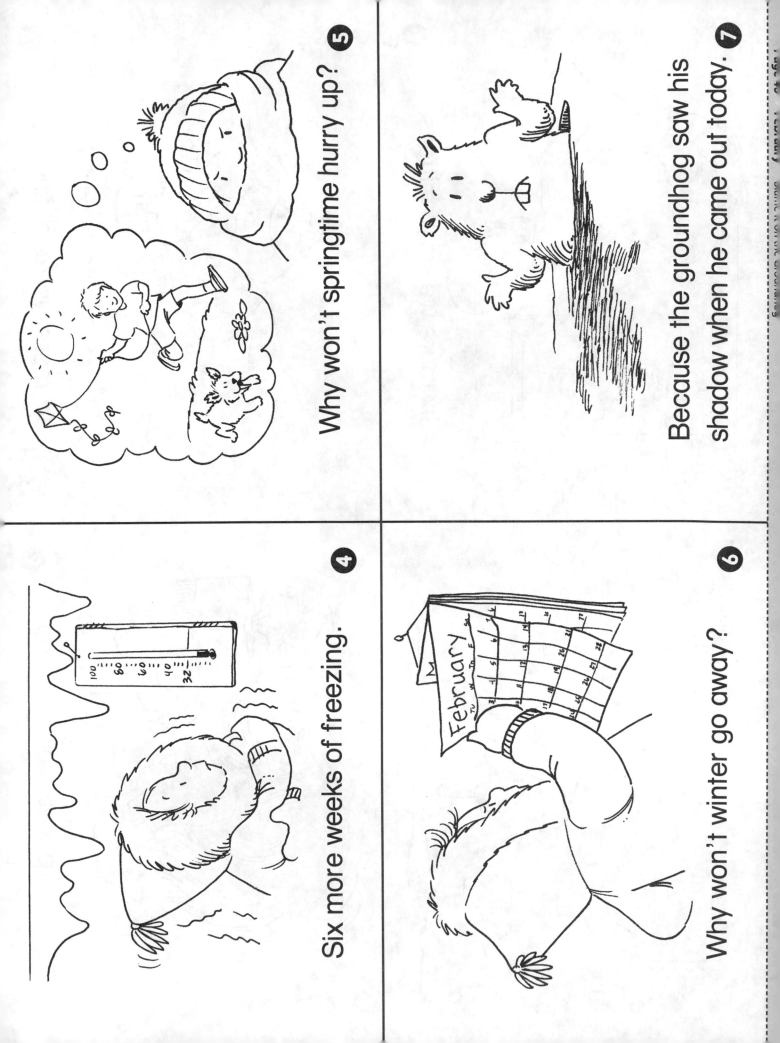

5 Why won't springtime hurry up?

7 Because the groundhog saw his shadow when he came out today.

4 Six more weeks of freezing.

6 Why won't winter go away?

Made With Love

Dad

1

What do you need to make a valentine?

2

You need a little bit of paper.

3

You need a little bit of paint.

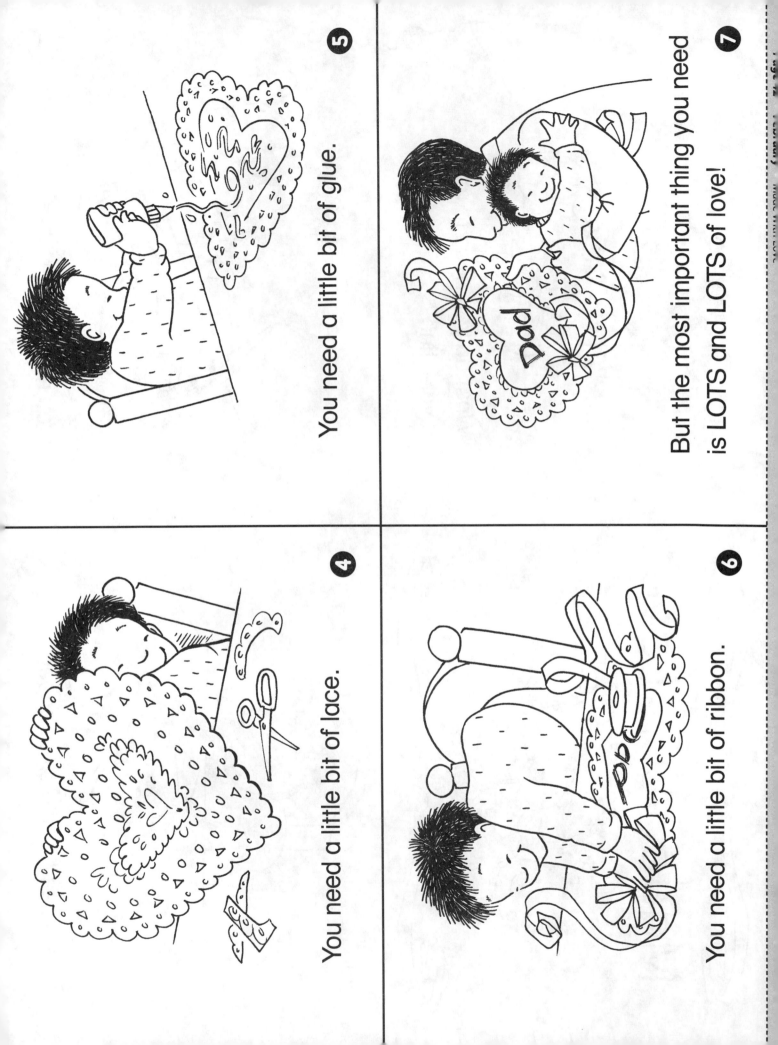

You need a little bit of glue.

But the most important thing you need is LOTS and LOTS of love!

4

6

You need a little bit of lace.

You need a little bit of ribbon.

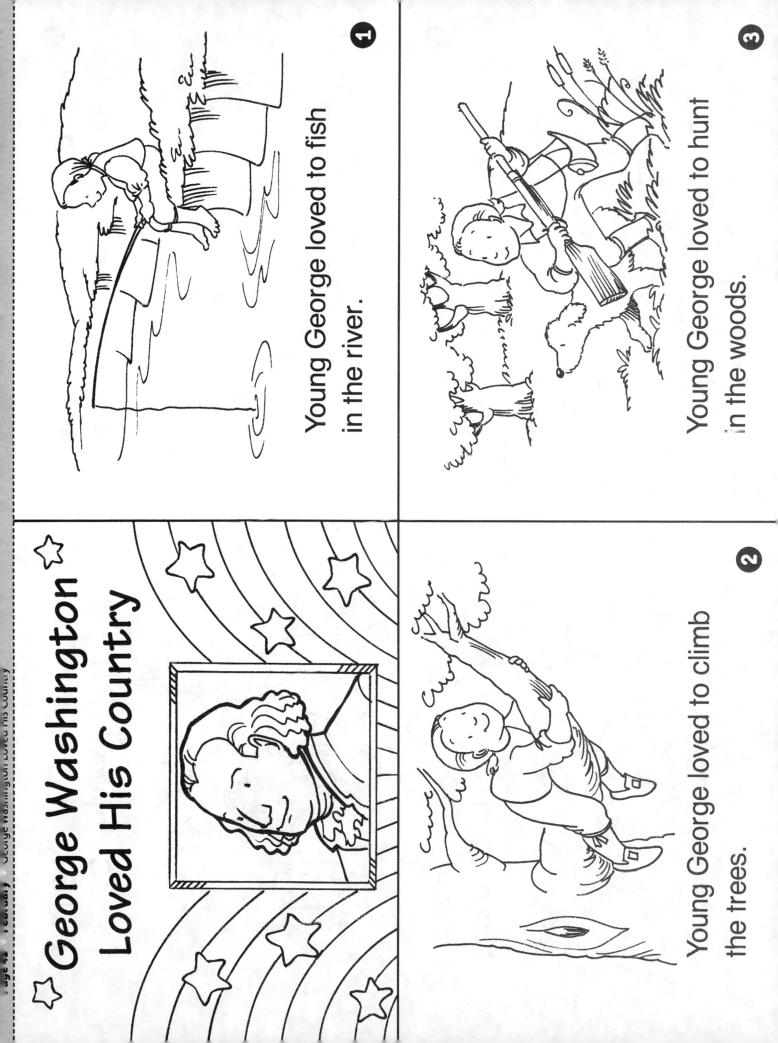

Young George loved to fish
in the river.

Young George loved to hunt
in the woods.

☆ George Washington ☆
Loved His Country

Young George loved to climb
the trees.

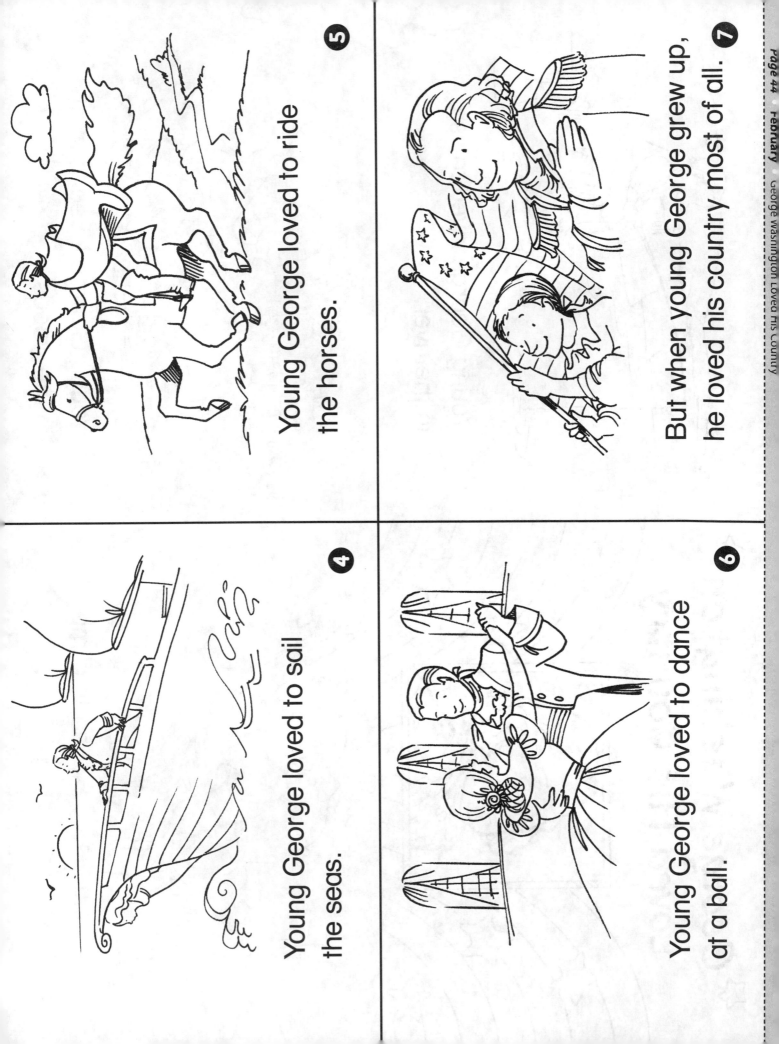

5

Young George loved to ride the horses.

4

Young George loved to sail the seas.

7

But when young George grew up, he loved his country most of all.

6

Young George loved to dance at a ball.

Have You Seen
My Pot of Gold?

1

Have you seen my pot of gold?

Go ask the cow.

2

Have you seen my pot of gold?

Go ask the horse.

3

Have you seen my pot of gold?

Go ask the pig.

Spring Is Here!

1

Sun is shining.
Spring is here!

2

Grass is growing.
Spring is here!

3

Flowers are blooming.
Spring is here!

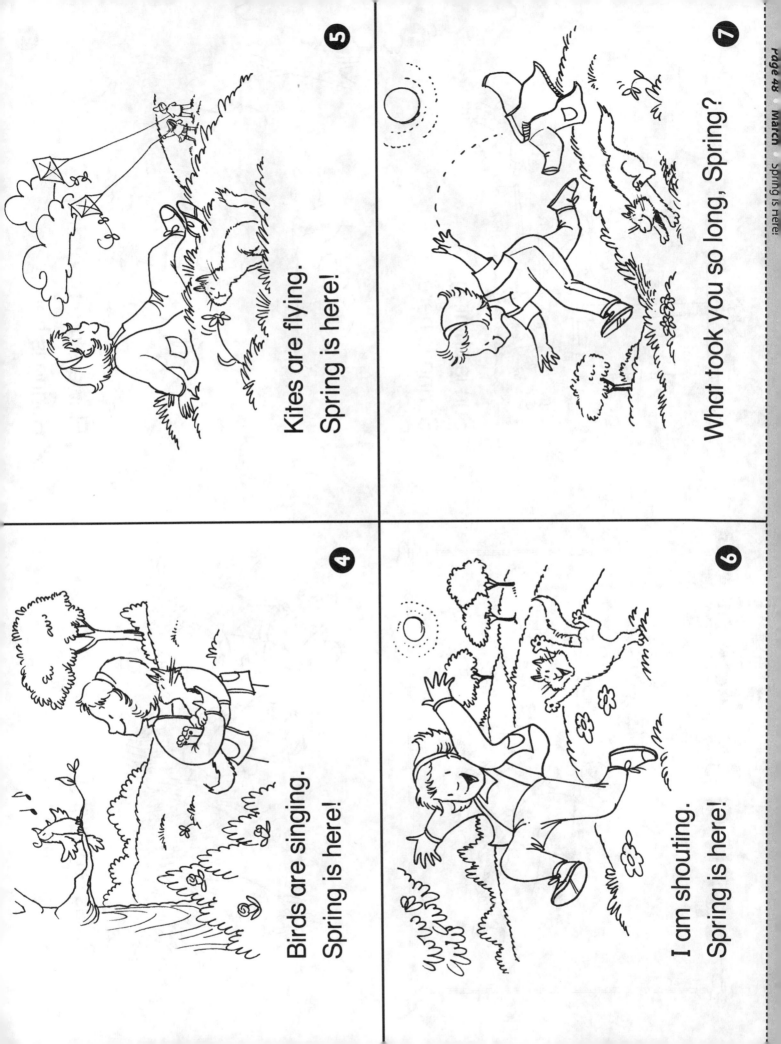

7

What took you so long, Spring?

5

Kites are flying.
Spring is here!

4

Birds are singing.
Spring is here!

6

I am shouting.
Spring is here!

1 Today I saw a rat chasing a cat,

2 a frog chasing a dog,

3 a goose chasing a moose,

Guess What I Saw Today!

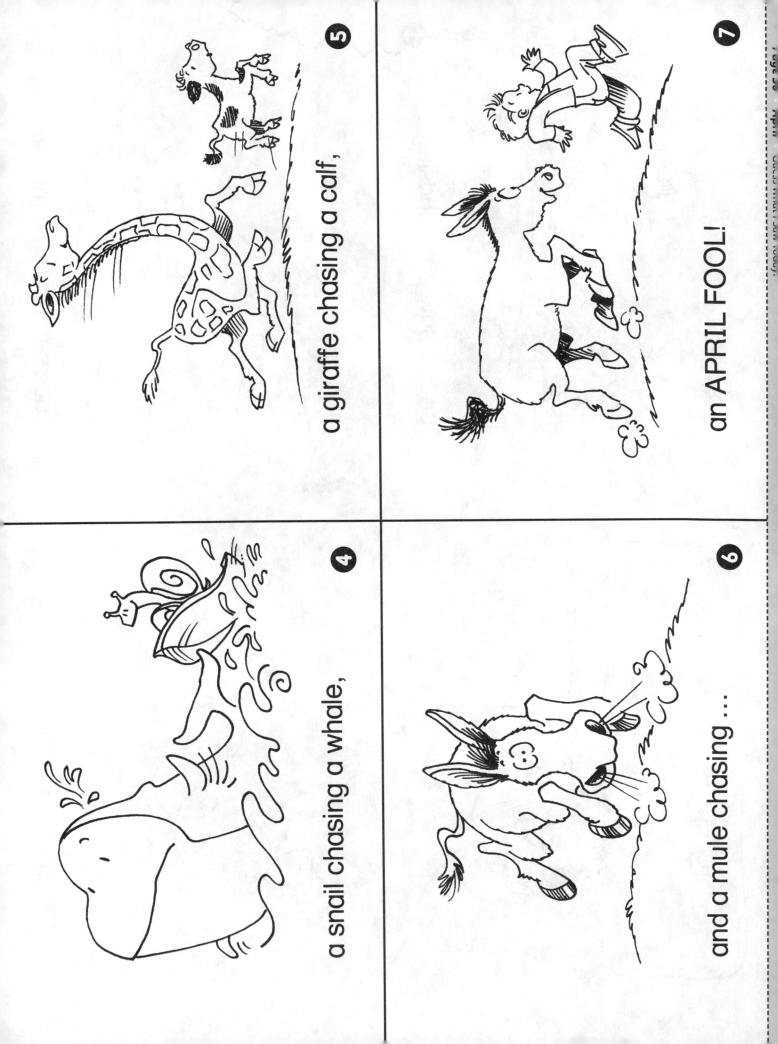

7

an APRIL FOOL!

5

a giraffe chasing a calf,

6

and a mule chasing ...

4

a snail chasing a whale,

Who Needs a Tree?

1

Who needs a tree?
Birds do.

2

Who needs a tree?
Squirrels do.

3

Who needs a tree?
Bees do.

Who needs a tree?
Bats do.

Who needs a tree?
I do!

Who needs a tree?
Caterpillars do.

Who needs a tree?
Raccoons do.

Be kind to friends with feathers.

1

Be kind to friends who bark.

Woof!

3

Be Kind to Furry Friends

Be kind to friends with fur.

2

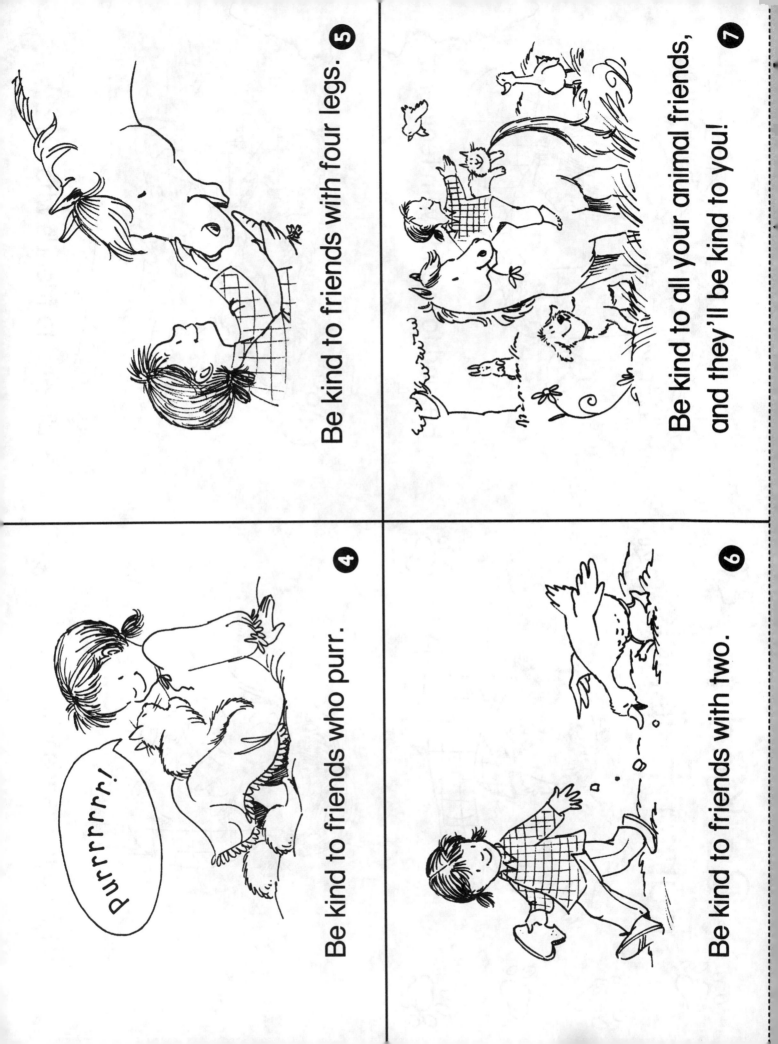

5

Be kind to friends with four legs.

7

Be kind to all your animal friends, and they'll be kind to you!

4

Purrrrrrr!

Be kind to friends who purr.

6

Be kind to friends with two.

Time for music.

1

Time for games.

3

Fiesta!

Time for dancing.

2

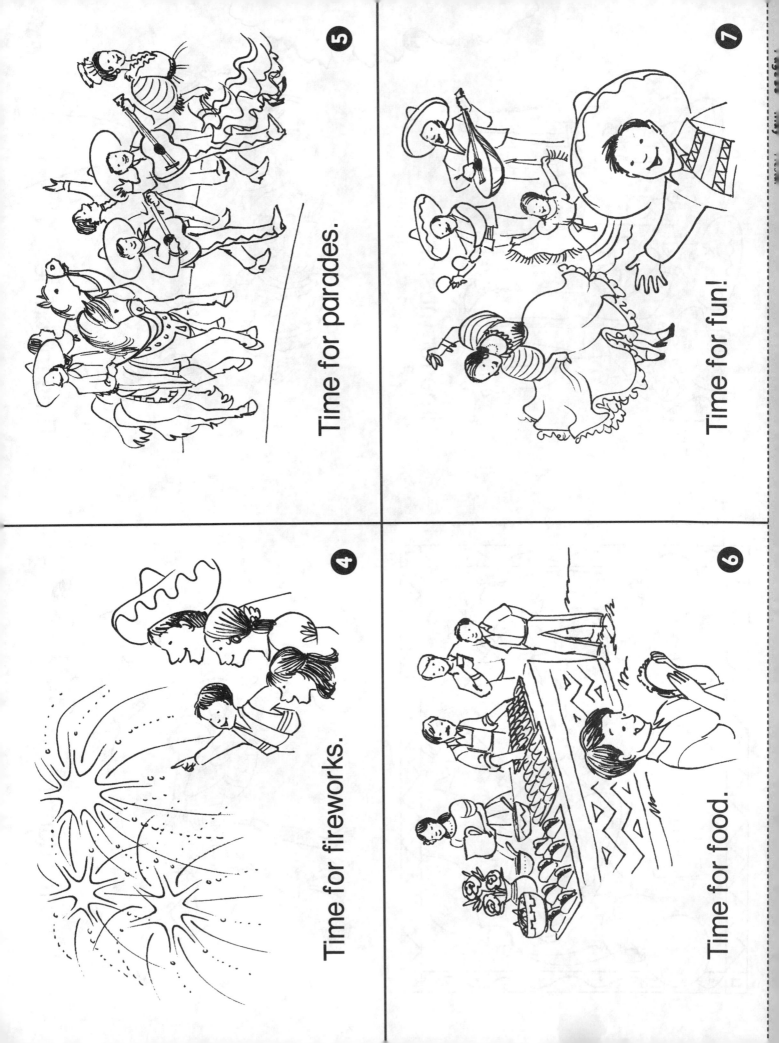

Time for parades.

Time for fun!

Time for fireworks.

Time for food.

1 What's red like a rose?

3 What's blue like the sea?

A June Mystery

2 What's white like a cloud?

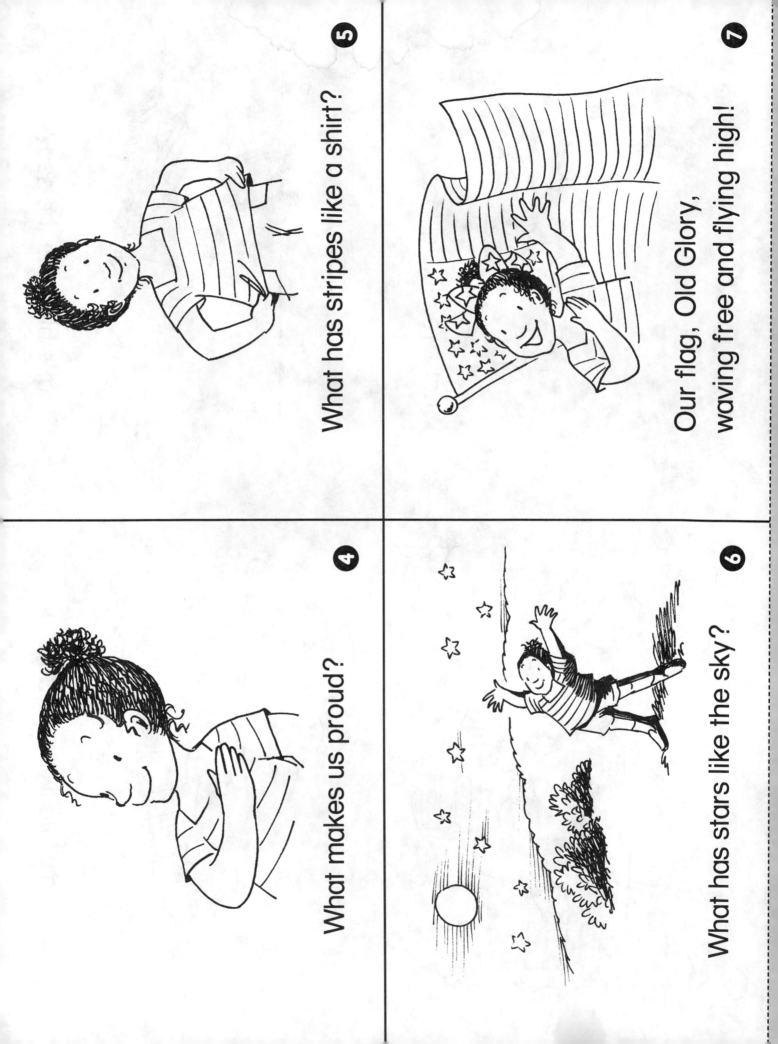

5

What has stripes like a shirt?

7

Our flag, Old Glory,
waving free and flying high!

4

What makes us proud?

6

What has stars like the sky?

1

Have a happy SUMMER!

Today is the last day of school.
Today is the last day of school.

3

Pack up your pencils and books.
Pack up your pencils and books.

School's Out!

(Sing to the tune of "The Farmer in the Dell")

2

Hip-hip-hooray, let's go and play!
Today is the last day of school.

5

Say good-bye to your friends.
Say good-bye to your friends.

7

Look out summer, here we come!

4

School is done, let's go have some fun!
Pack up your pencils and books.

6

Summer is here! See you next year!
Say good-bye to your friends.

Put on Your
Party Hat

Put on your party pants.

Put on your party socks.

Put on your party shirt.

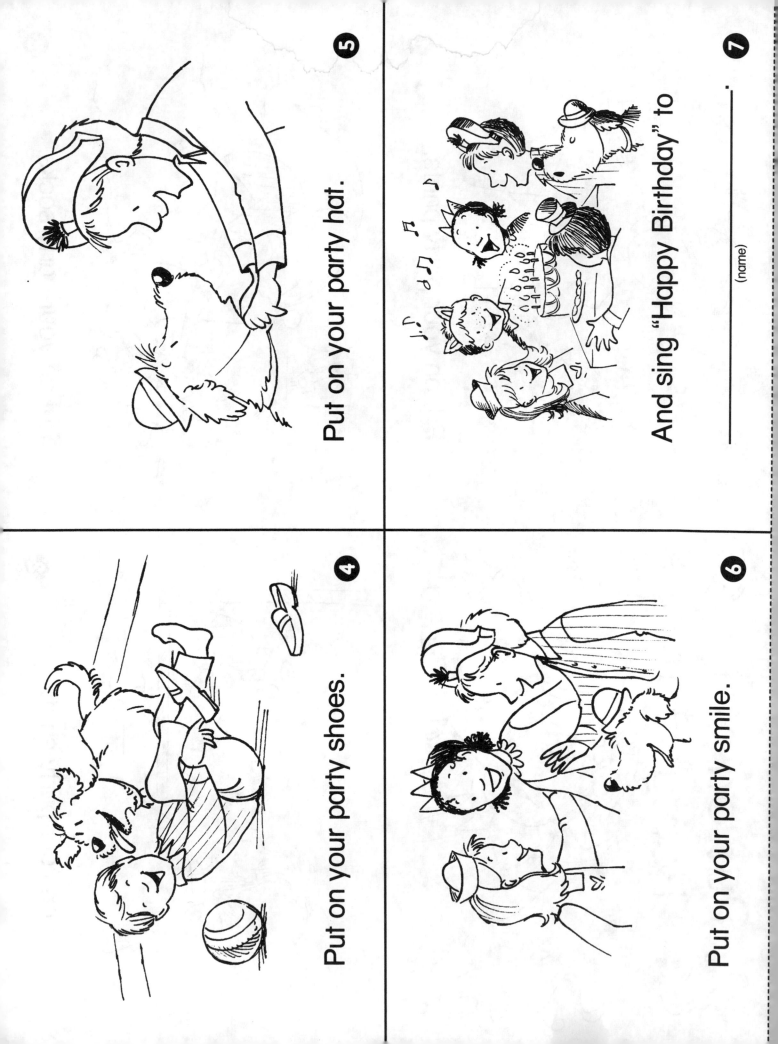

5

Put on your party hat.

7

And sing "Happy Birthday" to

_____.
(name)

4

Put on your party shoes.

6

Put on your party smile.

Gifts Are Great

1 I like gifts that come with bows.

2 I like gifts that come with tags.

3 I like gifts that come in boxes.

To: You! From: Me!

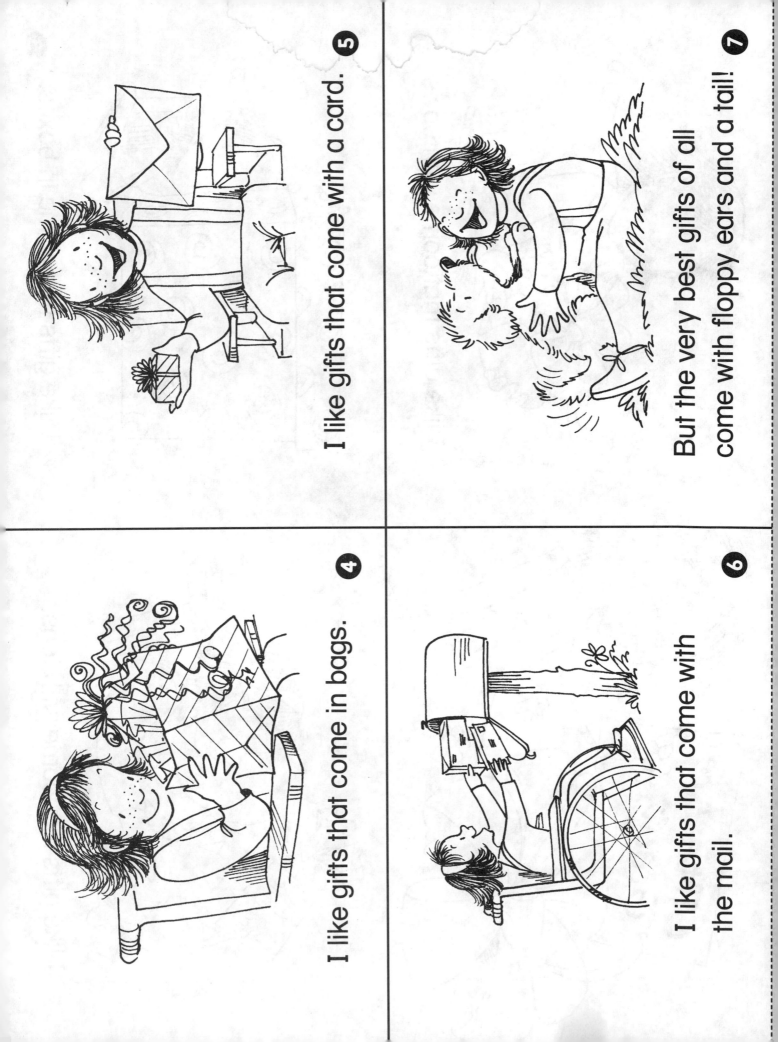

I like gifts that come in bags.

❹

I like gifts that come with a card.

❺

I like gifts that come with the mail.

❻

But the very best gifts of all come with floppy ears and a tail!

❼